The Science of Reading Decodable Curriculum: Phonemic Awareness, Decodable Readers, and Phonics Lessons Workbook for Grades Kindergarten, First Grade, Second Grade, and Third Grade

Dear Parents and Teachers,

We extend our heartfelt gratitude to each of you for choosing our Science of Reading curriculum. Your decision to invest in your child's education is commendable, and we are honored to be a part of their reading journey. At the heart of our curriculum lies the fundamental understanding of phonemic awareness, phonics, and the integration of decodable books, all of which are pivotal in fostering strong literacy skills in young readers. Phonemic awareness forms the basis of understanding how sounds work in words, while phonics provides the essential link between sounds and letters, empowering children to decode words with confidence.

We firmly believe that this curriculum serves as the crucial first step in your child's reading journey, laying down a solid foundation upon which further literacy skills can be built. The incorporation of decodable books ensures that children have access to texts that align closely with the phonics principles they are learning, facilitating a seamless transition from decoding to comprehension. As your child embarks on this exciting adventure of learning to read, rest assured that our curriculum is designed to support their growth every step of the way.

Should you have any questions or require further assistance regarding the curriculum or your child's progress, please do not hesitate to reach out to us at decodabletexts@gmail.com. We are here to support you and your child on this enriching journey towards literacy mastery. Once again, thank you for choosing our Science of Reading curriculum. Together, we can unlock the transformative power of reading in your child's life.

Warm regards,
Adam Free

TABLE OF CONTENTS

- **01** Short a set
- **02** Short o set
- **03** Short e set
- **04** Short u set
- **05** Short i set

Short a
Set 1

Phonemic Awareness

For this exercise, asks your student to blend each word together. Do not allow them to see any part of the word or book. This is an oral exercise.

Teacher: "Repeat after me.

c-a-t

caaaaaaat

cat"

(First, say each sound individually. Then blend them together, dragging out the middle "a" sound. Next, say the word.)

Phonemic Awareness

Now, repeat this same process for each of the words below.

c-a-t	caaaaaaaaat	cat
m-a-t	maaaaaaaat	mat

m-a-n
a-n-d
h-a-t
h-a-d
h-a-s
b-a-t
f-a-n
m-a-d
p-a-t
y-a-m

Phonemic Awareness

First, say each word. Next, ask students to (1) change the first letter of the word. Or (2) ask students to change the last letter of the word.

cat (Ex. fat, pat,) (Ex. cap, cam)

mat

man

and

hat

had

has

bat

fan

mad

pat

yam

Words

Ask your student to read each of the words and sentences.

cat	hat	sat
mat	man	and
the	a	bat

Sentences

1. The cat sat.
2. The man sat.
3. The man and cat sat.
4. The cat has a bat.
5. The man has a bat.

Story

The cat sat. The man sat. The cat and man sat. The cat has a bat. The man has a bat. The cat and man had a bat. The cat sat at the mat. The man sat at the mat. The cat and man sat at the mat.

Draw what happened in the story

Ask your student to read the following nonsense words from the box below. Though these are not real words, the goal is to get students to read them fluently and quickly. To accomplish this, you student may try as many times as possible within 3-5 minutes.

Silly Sentences

1. cav, gak, paj, mab, baf.
2. faf, lav, kam, tac, hav.
3. lat, pac, raf, vat, caz,
4. zax, jat, hap, fav, waj.
5. gan, jat, raz, kax, daf.
6. vab, yap, nams, vats.

Ask your student to spell and write the following words: cat, sat, hat, man, had, bat.

Short a
Set 2

Phonemic Awareness

For this exercise, asks your student to blend each word together. Do not allow them to see any part of the word or book. This is an oral exercise.

Teacher: "Repeat after me.
c-a-t
caaaaaaat
cat"

(First, say each sound individually. Then blend them together, dragging out the middle "a" sound. Next, say the word.)

Phonemic Awareness

Now, repeat this same process for each of the words below.

r-a-m   raaaaaam   ram
r-a-n   raaaaaan   ran
m-a-p
a-n-d
h-a-t
h-a-d
c-a-p
b-a-t
f-a-n
l-a-g
p-a-t
d-a-d

Phonemic Awareness

First, say each word. Next, ask students to (1) change the first letter of the word. Or (2) ask students to change the last letter of the word.

ram (Ex. Pam, jam) (Ex. rad, rap)

ran

map

and

hat

had

cap

bat

fan

lag

pat

dad

Words

Ask your student to read each of the words and sentences.

dad	ran	rat
ram	man	and
the	to	mat

Sentences

1. The rat ran.
2. The ram ran.
3. The rat and ram ran.
4. The rat ran to dad.
5. The ram ran to dad.

Story

The rat ran. The ram ran. The rat and ram ran. The rat ran to dad. The ram ran to dad. The rat and ram ran to dad. The rat and ram ran to the mat and sat. The rat and ram ran and sat at the mat.

Draw what happened in the story

Ask your student to read the following nonsense words from the box below. Though these are not real words, the goal is to get students to read them fluently and quickly. To accomplish this, you student may try as many times as possible within 3-5 minutes.

Silly Sentences

1. tav, vak, naj, rab, waf.
2. fav, laz, kac, tam, han.
3. wat, zac, rax, jat, baz,
4. nax, lat, zaz, cav, daj.
5. gaf, dat, faz, yax, baf.
6. dab, yaz, rafs, pav.

Ask your student to spell and write the following words: rat, ram, ran, dad, mat, sat.

Short a
Set 3

Phonemic Awareness

For this exercise, asks your student to blend each word together. Do not allow them to see any part of the word or book. This is an oral exercise.

Teacher: "Repeat after me.

c-a-t

caaaaaaat

cat"

(First, say each sound individually. Then blend them together, dragging out the middle "a" sound. Next, say the word.)

Phonemic Awareness

Now, repeat this same process for each of the words below.

c-a-b   caaaaaab   cab
h-a-d   haaaaaad   had
r-a-g
a-t
h-a-m
h-a-d
S-a-m
D-a-n
f-a-n
l-a-g
p-a-d
d-a-b

Phonemic Awareness

First, say each word. Next, ask students to (1) change the first letter of the word. Or (2) ask students to change the last letter of the word.

cab (Ex. tab, lab) (Ex. can, cap)
had
rag
mat
ham
had
Sam
Dan
fan
lag
pad

Words

Ask your student to read each of the words and sentences.

Sam	**Dan**	**rat**
at	**man**	**and**
fan	**van**	**a**

Sentences

1. **Sam had a van.**
2. **Dan had a fat rat.**
3. **Sam had a ham.**
4. **Dan had a fan.**
5. **Sam is a man.**

Story

Sam had a van. Dan had a fat rat. Sam had a ham. Dan had a fan. Sam is a man. Dan is a man. Sam and Dan had a fan. Sam and Dan had a ham. Sam and Dan had a van. Sam and Dan had Dad.

Draw what happened in the story

Ask your student to read the following nonsense words from the box below. Though these are not real words, the goal is to get students to read them fluently and quickly. To accomplish this, you student may try as many times as possible within 3-5 minutes.

Silly Sentences

1. **tag, vas, waz, bac, lan.**
2. **nam, yaz, pak, rac, wag.**
3. **waz, gad, jas, tam.**
4. **pap, bagz, lax, wats.**
5. **sads, laz, las, ams.**
6. **ats, avs, lats, paps, acs.**

Ask your student to spell and write the following words: Sam, van, had, ham, Dan, fan.

Short a
Set 4

Phonemic Awareness

For this exercise, asks your student to blend each word together. Do not allow them to see any part of the word or book. This is an oral exercise.

Teacher: "Repeat after me.

c-a-t

caaaaaaat

cat"

(First, say each sound individually. Then, blend them together, dragging out the middle "a" sound. Next, say the word.)

Phonemic Awareness

Now, repeat this same process for each of the words below.

f-a-s-t   faaaaaast   fast
v-a-n   vaaaaaan   van
b-a-t
r-a-t
P-a-t
G-a-b
g-a-s
c-a-b
l-a-s-t
s-a-d
b-a-d

Phonemic Awareness

First, say each word. Next, ask students to (1) change the first letter of the word. Or (2) ask students to change the last letter of the word.

fast (Ex. past) (Ex. task)

van

bat

rat

Pat

Gab

gas

cab

last

sad

bad

Words

Ask your student to read each of the words and sentences.

fast	is	Pat
van	Gab	sat
bat	gas	bad

Sentences

1. The van is fast.
2. Pat is fast.
3. The bat is fast.
4. The van is fast.
5. Gab is fast.

Story

A van, Gab, Pat, and a bat ran. The van is fast. The van had gas. Gab is fast. The bat is fast. Pat was sad. Pat ran. Pat is last. Gab ran back to Pat. Gab and Pat sat. Gab and Pat sat at the mat.

Draw what happened in the story

Ask your student to read the following nonsense words from the box below. Though these are not real words, the goal is to get students to read them fluently and quickly. To accomplish this, you student may try as many times as possible within 3-5 minutes.

Silly Sentences

1. **pag, vav, wac, aps, san.**
2. **nas, yad, das, fas, abs.**
3. **zad, rad, rads, tav, ac.**
4. **babs, zac, hak, ams.**
5. **cav, vac, lav, aft, jan.**
6. **naj, jaj, wam, paps, vam.**

Ask your student to spell and write the following words: van, Gab, Pat, bat, sad, mat.

Short a
Set 5

Phonemic Awareness

For this exercise, asks your student to blend each word together. Do not allow them to see any part of the word or book. This is an oral exercise.

Teacher: "Repeat after me.

c-a-t

caaaaaaat

cat"

(First, say each sound individually. Then, blend them together, dragging out the middle "a" sound. Next, say the word.)

Phonemic Awareness

Now, repeat this same process for each of the words below.

n-a-p naaaaaap nap
j-a-m jaaaaaam jam
r-a-p
b-a-ck
s-a-ck
h-a-s
l-a-d
J-a-ck
z-a-p
c-a-t

Phonemic Awareness

First, say each word. Next, ask students to (1) change the first letter of the word. Or (2) ask students to change the last letter of the word.

nap (Ex. tap, lap) (Ex. nag, nat)
jam
rap
back
sack
has
lad
Jack
zap
cat

Words

Ask your student to read each of the words and sentences.

nap	Jack	in
sack	had	jam
back	by	rap

Sentences

1. The cat had a nap.
2. The cat had a nap in the van.
3. The cat had a nap in the back.
4. Jack sat in the back.

Story

The cat had a nap. The cat had a nap in the van. The cat sat at the back of the van. Jack sat by the cat. The cat had a nap in the sack. The cat had a nap by the jam. Jack sat by the cat.

Draw what happened in the story

Ask your student to read the following nonsense words from the box below. Though these are not real words, the goal is to get students to read them fluently and quickly. To accomplish this, you student may try as many times as possible within 3-5 minutes.

Silly Sentences

1. asp, vat, wan, bav, cads.
2. nast, pafs, kap, zan, paf.
3. zat, laps, jas, bap, kat.
4. nams, zax, yast, mas.
5. nas, lat, vam, waz, rax.
6. jan, zaz, waz, zas, yat.

Ask your student to spell and write the following words: nap, jam, had, van, sat, cat

Short o
Set 1

Phonemic Awareness

For this exercise, asks your student to blend each word together. Do not allow them to see any part of the word or book. This is an oral exercise.

Teacher: "Repeat after me.
t-o-p
tooooooop
top"

(First, say each sound individually. Then, blend them together, dragging out the middle "o" sound. Next, say the word.)

Phonemic Awareness

Now, repeat this same process for each of the words below.

f-o-x   foooooox   fox
h-o-p   hoooooop   hop
g-o-t
h-o-t
n-o-t
b-o-x
t-o-t
b-o-t
d-o-t
l-o-t
l-o-ck
m-o-ck

Phonemic Awareness

First, say each word. Next, ask students to (1) change the first letter of the word. Or (2) ask students to change the last letter of the word.

fox   (Ex. tox, rox) (fot, fon)
hop
got
hot
not
box
tot
bot
dot
lot
lock

Words

Ask your student to read each of the words and sentences.

fox	hot	was
hop	log	lock
stop	not	dock

Sentences

1. The fox can hop.
2. The fox got hot.
3. The fox got on a log.
4. The fox did not.
5. The dock has a lock.

Story

The fox can hop. The fox can hop on a log. The fox got hot. The fox has a top. The fox has a lock. The fox is at the dock. The dock has a lock. The fox ran past the dock. Do not stop. Do not sob. The fox did not.

Draw what happened in the story

Ask your student to read the following nonsense words from the box below. Though these are not real words, the goal is to get students to read them fluently and quickly. To accomplish this, you student may try as many times as possible within 3-5 minutes.

Silly Sentences

1. mot, tam, cov, ros, mok.
2. moz, tox, wof, pab, pob.
3. rom, gop, vot, jon, mod.
4. woc, wac, vof, lon, lod.
5. bom, dov, zop, fob, ogs.
6. jost, kof, daf, wod, dof.

Ask your student to spell and write the following words: not, hot, pot, fox, hop, bot

Short o Set 2

Phonemic Awareness

For this exercise, asks your student to blend each word together. Do not allow them to see any part of the word or book. This is an oral exercise.

Teacher: "Repeat after me.

t-o-p

tooooooop

top"

(First, say each sound individually. Then, blend them together, dragging out the middle "o" sound. Next, say the word.)

Phonemic Awareness

Now, repeat this same process for each of the words below.

c-o-b   cooob   cob
j-o-b   jooob   job
f-o-g
b-o-t
n-o-d
r-o-d
m-o-p
t-o-p
R-o-n
c-o-t
t-o-t

Phonemic Awareness

First, say each word. Next, ask students to (1) change the first letter of the word. Or (2) ask students to change the last letter of the word.

cob   (Ex. cot, con) (mob, fob)
job
fog
bot
nod
rod
mop
top
Ron
cot
tot

Words

Ask your student to read each of the words and sentences.

bot	hot	was
fog	in	lock
stop	is	dock

Sentences

1. Ron is a bot.
2. Bon is the bot's mom.
3. Ron and Bon ran in the fog.
4. The fog is hot.
5. Ron and Bon ran into a log.

Story

Ron is a bot. The bot has a mom. Bon is the bot's mom. Ron and Bon can jog. Ron can jog to the job. Mom can jog to a hog. Ron and mom can jog to pop. Pop is Ron's dad. Pop, Mom, and Ron jog to the bot tot.

Draw what happened in the story

Ask your student to read the following nonsense words from the box below. Though these are not real words, the goal is to get students to read them fluently and quickly. To accomplish this, you student may try as many times as possible within 3-5 minutes.

Silly Sentences

1. mox, zam, lok, fon, tob.
2. maz, lox, vob, hod, wot.
3. rog, lop, vat, jom, cos.
4. tof, sot, son, los, bam.
5. hod, zoc, oz, oms, ags.
6. osc, rof, gan, woz, fod.

Ask your student to spell and write the following words: bot, mom, pop, Ron, fog, tot.

Short o
Set 3

Phonemic Awareness

For this exercise, asks your student to blend each word together. Do not allow them to see any part of the word or book. This is an oral exercise.

Teacher: "Repeat after me.

t-o-p

tooooooop

top"

(First, say each sound individually. Then, blend them together, dragging out the middle "o" sound. Next, say the word.)

Phonemic Awareness

Now, repeat this same process for each of the words below.

m-o-m	mooom	mom
t-o-m	tooom	tom
p-o-p		
p-o-t		
b-o-x		
r-o-t		
c-o-p		
d-o-t		
R-o-n		
m-o-m		
l-o-t		

Phonemic Awareness

First, say each word. Next, ask students to (1) change the first letter of the word. Or (2) ask students to change the last letter of the word.

mom   (Ex. Tom, rom) (Ex. mop)
tom
pop
pot
box
rot
cop
dot
Ron
mom
lot

Words

Ask your student to read each of the words and sentences.

mom	Tom	of
got	hot	
pop	logs	

Sentences

1. Mom got pop a pot of hogs.
2. Mom got Tom a lot of logs.
3. Mom got the cop a dog bot.
4. Mom got the fox a rod.
5. Mom got the pot hot.

Story

Mom got pop a pot of hogs.
Mom got Tom a lot of logs.
Mom got the cop a dog bot.
Mom got the fox a hot rod.
Mom has a top in a pot. Mom has the pot in a box. Mom did not stop. Mom has the top job.

Draw what happened in the story

Ask your student to read the following nonsense words from the box below. Though these are not real words, the goal is to get students to read them fluently and quickly. To accomplish this, you student may try as many times as possible within 3-5 minutes.

Silly Sentences

1. **gox, zom, lod, oms, tav.**
2. **mov, von, vam, hoc, jop.**
3. **gop, laz, lox, jom, nax.**
4. **joz, ams, oms, mas, mos.**
5. **haf, zaf, maf, taf, raf.**
6. **foz, daz, goc, los, faf.**

Ask your student to spell and write the following words: mom, top, job, box, pot, hogs

Short o
Set 4

Phonemic Awareness

For this exercise, asks your student to blend each word together. Do not allow them to see any part of the word or book. This is an oral exercise.

Teacher: "Repeat after me.

t-o-p

tooooooop

top"

(First, say each sound individually. Then, blend them together, dragging out the middle "o" sound. Next, say the word.)

Phonemic Awareness

Now, repeat this same process for each of the words below.

B-o-b   Booob   Bob
m-o-p   mooop   mop
o-d-d
d-o-g
c-o-p
p-o-p
s-o-ck
R-o-b
r-o-ck
c-o-t
d-o-t
r-o-m

Phonemic Awareness

First, say each word. Next, ask students to (1) change the first letter of the word. Or (2) ask students to change the last letter of the word.

Bob   (Ex. cob, vop) (Ex. bop, bov)
mop
odd
dog
cop
pop
sock
Rob
rock
cot
dot

Words

Ask your student to read each of the words and sentences.

Bob	**cop**	**Rob**
mop	**dog**	**rock**
odd	**pop**	**cot**

Sentences

1. **Bob has a dog.**
2. **The dog is a cop.**
3. **The dog is not.**
4. **The dog ran back at Bob.**
5. **Bob ran at the dog.**

Story

Bob has a dog. The dog is a cop. Bob ran at the dog cop. Bob is odd. The dog is not. The dog ran to a cot and rock. Bob ran at a mop. The dog ran back at Bob. Bob ran at the dog.

Draw what happened in the story

Ask your student to read the following nonsense words from the box below. Though these are not real words, the goal is to get students to read them fluently and quickly. To accomplish this, you student may try as many times as possible within 3-5 minutes.

Silly Sentences

1. **zot, moz, dab, bod, vots.**
2. **movs, jom, tog, wons.**
3. **wan, zoc, vot, yom, hom.**
4. **jas, gog, non, cof, lops.**
5. **rogs, fom, lac, von, bab.**
6. **fof, dac, hol, bop, obs.**

Ask your student to spell and write the following words: Bob, cot, cop, mop, cot, not.

Short o
Set 5

Phonemic Awareness

For this exercise, asks your student to blend each word together. Do not allow them to see any part of the word or book. This is an oral exercise.

Teacher: "Repeat after me.
t-o-p
toooooop
top"

(First, say each sound individually. Then, blend them together, dragging out the middle "o" sound. Next, say the word.)

Phonemic Awareness

Now, repeat this same process for each of the words below.

T-o-t-s　toooots　tots
m-o-ss　moooos　mos
l-o-s-t
d-o-t-s
l-o-t
n-o-d
h-o-g
p-o-d
f-o-x
b-o-ss
c-o-t-s

Phonemic Awareness

First, say each word. Next, ask students to (1) change the first letter of the word. Or (2) ask students to change the last letter of the word.

Tot   (Ex. lot, not) (toc, tog)
moss
lost
dots
lot
nod
hog
pod
fox
boss
cots

Words

Ask your student to read each of the words and sentences.

tots	dots	hog
moss	of	pod
lost	nod	to

Sentences

1. The tots ran to the moss.
2. The tots got lost.
3. The tots nod at the fox.
4. the tots sat on dots.
5. The tots nod at the fox.

Story

The tots ran to the moss. The tots got lost. The tots ran and ran. The tots pass a fox. The tots nod at the fox. The tots pass a hog. The tots nod at a hog. The tots pass a pod of dots. The tots sat on the dots. The tots ran to mom and pop.

Draw what happened in the story

Ask your student to read the following nonsense words from the box below. Though these are not real words, the goal is to get students to read them fluently and quickly. To accomplish this, you student may try as many times as possible within 3-5 minutes.

Silly Sentences

1. **toz, zam, bos, ras, sot.**
2. **pofs, mast, rops, san.**
3. **fod, mam, dod, yom.**
4. **pap, raz, pox, mot, gad.**
5. **fots, vost, pam, locs.**
6. **bab, gog, tat, vov, zoz.**

Ask your student to spell and write the following words: dot, pod, pop, hog, mom, lost

___ ___ ___

___ ___ ___

___ ___ ___

___ ___ ___

___ ___ ___

___ ___ ___ ___

Short e
Set 1

Phonemic Awareness

For this exercise, asks your student to blend each word together. Do not allow them to see any part of the word or book. This is an oral exercise.

Teacher: "Repeat after me.

m-e-n

meeeeeen

men"

(First, say each sound individually. Then, blend them together, dragging out the middle "e" sound. Next, say the word.)

Phonemic Awareness

Now, repeat this same process for each of the words below.

b-e-d   beeeeed   bed
d-e-n   deeeeen   den
r-e-d
t-e-n
h-e-n
v-e-s-t
n-e-t
e-gg
p-e-ck
b-e-n-d
l-e-g

Phonemic Awareness

First, say each word. Next, ask students to (1) change the first letter of the word. Or (2) ask students to change the last letter of the word.

bed

den

red

ten

hen

vest

net

egg

peck

bend

leg

Words

Ask your student to read each of the words and sentences.

hen	red	peck
bed	vest	ten
bend	egg	leg

Sentences

1. The hen sat in bed.
2. The hen bends to peck the red net.
3. The hen ran to pet the eggs.
4. The hen had ten red eggs.

Story

The hen sat in bed. The hen fell on a red net. The hen bends to peck the red net. The hen ran to pet the eggs. The hen had ten red eggs. The hen set the eggs in the den. The hen sets the eggs in the bed. The hen went back to bed.

Draw what happened in the story

Ask your student to read the following nonsense words from the box below. Though these are not real words, the goal is to get students to read them fluently and quickly. To accomplish this, you student may try as many times as possible within 3-5 minutes.

Silly Sentences

1. **het, wep, lek, kem, ted.**
2. **fet, hez, zed, heb, wep.**
3. **yec, nes, gec, fen, bes.**
4. **les, nen, pel, nem, ret.**
5. **tet, jem, teg, hez, lems.**
6. **jez, sed, heg, lep, ket.**

Ask your student to spell and write the following words: hen, bed, red, set, net, went

Short e
Set 2

Phonemic Awareness

For this exercise, asks your student to blend each word together. Do not allow them to see any part of the word or book. This is an oral exercise.

Teacher: "Repeat after me.

m-e-n

meeeeeen

men"

(First, say each sound individually. Then, blend them together, dragging out the middle "e" sound. Next, say the word.)

Phonemic Awareness

Now, repeat this same process for each of the words below.

K-e-n   keeeeen   ken
v-e-t   veeeeet   vet
w-e-ll
b-e-ll
y-e-ll
p-e-n
w-e-t
m-e-ss
j-e-ff
m-e-n
s-e-t

Phonemic Awareness

First, say each word. Next, ask students to (1) change the first letter of the word. Or (2) ask students to change the last letter of the word.

Ken (Ex. ten) (Ex. ken)
vet
well
bell
yell
pen
wet
mess
jeff
men
set

Words

Ask your student to read each of the words and sentences.

bell	well	yell
wet	mess	Jeff
Ken	set	was

Sentences

1. The bell is a wet mess.
2. Jeff bet he can get the bell in a net.
3. Jeff asks Ken to help.
4. The bell fell to the bed.
5. Jeff and Ken sell the bell.

Story

The bell is a wet mess. Jeff bet he can get the bell in a net. Jeff asks Ken to help. The bell fell to the bed. The bell is not well. Jeff yells. Ken yells. The bell is wet. Jeff and Ken sell the bell. Yes, the men sell the bell.

Draw what happened in the story

Ask your student to read the following nonsense words from the box below. Though these are not real words, the goal is to get students to read them fluently and quickly. To accomplish this, you student may try as many times as possible within 3-5 minutes.

Silly Sentences

1. hed, paf, woc, meg, len.
2. wan, fep, vog, nem, sen.
3. kag, vot, hez, jep, daf.
4. jek, hoc, yem, bas, sog.
5. et, pes, sep, gaf, em.
6. res, wef, vad, zek, lox.

Ask your student to spell and write the following words: wet, bet, get, set, bed, help

Short e
Set 3

Phonemic Awareness

For this exercise, asks your student to blend each word together. Do not allow them to see any part of the word or book. This is an oral exercise.

Teacher: "Repeat after me.

m-e-n

meeeeeen

men"

(First, say each sound individually. Then, blend them together, dragging out the middle "e" sound. Next, say the word.)

Phonemic Awareness

Now, repeat this same process for each of the words below.

p-e-t   peeeeet   pet
b-e-s-t   beeeeest   best
m-e-t
h-e-n
p-e-n
e-n-d
d-e-n
p-e-p
w-e-b
e-l-k
b-e-t

Phonemic Awareness

First, say each word. Next, ask students to (1) change the first letter of the word. Or (2) ask students to change the last letter of the word.

pet (Ex. set) (Ex. pen)
best
met
hen
pen
end
den
pep
web
elk
bet

Words

Ask your student to read each of the words and sentences.

pet	hen	end
best	pen	den
met	web	elk

Sentences

1. I had the best pet.
2. It is a red hen in a den.
3. Jeff met an elk by a pen.
4. Tess had the best pet.
5. Ted sat by ten webs.

Story

I had the best pet. It is a red hen in a den. The hen pecks at a leg. Jeff had the best pet. Jeff met an elk by a pen. Tess had the best pet. Tess and Ted sat by a web. Tess and Ted had the best pet yet. The vet met the pets by the den.

Draw what happened in the story

Ask your student to read the following nonsense words from the box below. Though these are not real words, the goal is to get students to read them fluently and quickly. To accomplish this, you student may try as many times as possible within 3-5 minutes.

Silly Sentences

1. **jed, daf, voc, neg, kon.**
2. **joc, zod, bap, nef, des.**
3. **las, wab, hoz, fep, deg.**
4. **mez, heds, vep, lof.**
5. **lep, seg, vex, paf, em.**
6. **rez, faz, hej, tex, het.**

Ask your student to spell and write the following words: elk, hen, pen, den, pet, best.

Short e
Set 4

Phonemic Awareness

For this exercise, asks your student to blend each word together. Do not allow them to see any part of the word or book. This is an oral exercise.

Teacher: "Repeat after me.
m-e-n
meeeeeen
men"

(First, say each sound individually. Then, blend them together, dragging out the middle "e" sound. Next, say the word.)

Phonemic Awareness

Now, repeat this same process for each of the words below.

J-e-t   jeeeet   jet
B-e-n   Beeen   ben
J-e-n
l-e-g
f-e-d
p-e-p
w-e-n-t
w-e-b
n-e-t
r-e-d
b-e-s-t

Phonemic Awareness

First, say each word. Next, ask students to (1) change the first letter of the word. Or (2) ask students to change the last letter of the word.

Jet   (Ex. het) (Ex. jed)
Ben
Jen
leg
fed
pep
went
web
net
red
best

Words

Ask your student to read each of the words and sentences.

into	**Ben**	**pep**
jet	**leg**	**went**
Jen	**fed**	**net**

Sentences

1. **Ben had a red jet.**
2. **The jet had a pep.**
3. **Ben went on the jet.**
4. **Jen went on the jet.**
5. **The jet went into a net.**

Story

Ben had a red jet. The jet had a fast pep. Ben went on the jet. Jen went on the jet. The jet went fast. The jet went into a net. The jet went into a web. The jet went into a red bell. The jet went to the end. The jet is the best.

Draw what happened in the story

Ask your student to read the following nonsense words from the box below. Though these are not real words, the goal is to get students to read them fluently and quickly. To accomplish this, you student may try as many times as possible within 3-5 minutes.

Silly Sentences

1. jej, tet, vev, nen, fef.
2. het, zad, dax, pel, jel.
3. hos, wol, vad, fez, tec.
4. zes, eps, joc, bes, det.
5. heb, voz, ret, ost, est.
6. jec, zoj, wasc, sost, zep.

Ask your student to spell and write the following words: jet, fed, leg, end, Jen, went.

Short e
Set 5

Phonemic Awareness

For this exercise, asks your student to blend each word together. Do not allow them to see any part of the word or book. This is an oral exercise.

Teacher: "Repeat after me.

m-e-n

meeeeeen

men"

(First, say each sound individually. Then, blend them together, dragging out the middle "e" sound. Next, say the word.)

Phonemic Awareness

Now, repeat this same process for each of the words below.

h-e-l-p
t-e-s-t
L-e-n
n-e-t
m-e-n
t-e-n
w-e-n-t
b-e-n-t
r-e-s-t
b-e-d
m-e-t

Phonemic Awareness

First, say each word. Next, ask students to (1) change the first letter of the word. Or (2) ask students to change the last letter of the word.

help   (Ex. felp) (Ex. heln)
test
Len
net
men
ten
went
bent
rest
bed
met

Words

Ask your student to read each of the words and sentences.

Len	test	met
net	off	bent
help	ten	rest

Sentences

1. Len went to rest in a bed.
2. Len fell in a net.
3. Ten men went to help Len.
4. The ten men bent to help let off the net.
5. Len let the men help.

Story

Len went to rest in bed. Len fell in a net. Ten hens went to help Len. The ten hens bent to help Len off the net. Len let the hens help. Len went to bed. The hens went to the jet. The hens went to help a vet.

Draw what happened in the story

Ask your student to read the following nonsense words from the box below. Though these are not real words, the goal is to get students to read them fluently and quickly. To accomplish this, you student may try as many times as possible within 3-5 minutes.

Silly Sentences

1. **hed, jem, tof, les, wev.**
2. **vob, mef, lac, bov, zep.**
3. **kex, wan, lat, zes, heg.**
4. **bes, det, bom, rel, nel.**
5. **wab, kag, zos, wev, bok.**
6. **seg, pel, rex, pol, wat.**

Ask your student to spell and write the following words: bed, vet, men, net, Len, rest.

Short u
Set 1

Phonemic Awareness

For this exercise, asks your student to blend each word together. Do not allow them to see any part of the word or book. This is an oral exercise.

Teacher: "Repeat after me.

b-u-g

buuuuuuug

bug"

(First, say each sound individually. Then, blend them together, dragging out the middle "u" sound. Next, say the word.)

Phonemic Awareness

Now, repeat this same process for each of the words below.

b-u-g   buuuuug bug
r-u-g   ruuuuug rug
r-u-b
h-u-g
m-u-d
g-u-m
h-u-t
c-u-t
r-u-n
c-u-p
s-u-n

Phonemic Awareness

First, say each word. Next, ask students to (1) change the first letter of the word. Or (2) ask students to change the last letter of the word.

bug   (Ex. kug) (Ex. bud)

rug

rub

hug

mud

gum

hut

cut

run

cup

sun

Words

Ask your student to read each of the words and sentences.

bug	was	sun
mud	but	hunt
the	hut	fun

Sentences

1. The bug went on the bus.
2. The bug went in the hunt.
3. The bug sat in the sun.
4. The bug hums.
5. The bug had fun.

Story

The bug went on the bus. The bug went in the hut. The bug runs in the sun. The bug hums in the mud. The bug had fun. The bug had to hunt for nuts. The bug dug for gum. The bug had fun.

Draw what happened in the story

Ask your student to read the following nonsense words from the box below. Though these are not real words, the goal is to get students to read them fluently and quickly. To accomplish this, you student may try as many times as possible within 3-5 minutes.

Silly Sentences

1. lum, pud, fuz, wuv, tun.
2. jum, fuv, lup, zuc, rux.
3. sup, duv, nux, wum, hup.
4. yus, cuj, juk, mup, rus.
5. vum, yud, wuk, zut, ust.
6. vuf, guv, lut, rup, gus.

Ask your student to spell and write the following words: run, bug, hut, fun, mud, hunt.

Short u Set 2

Phonemic Awareness

For this exercise, asks your student to blend each word together. Do not allow them to see any part of the word or book. This is an oral exercise.

Teacher: "Repeat after me.
b-u-g
buuuuuuug
bug"

(First, say each sound individually. Then, blend them together, dragging out the middle "u" sound. Next, say the word.)

Phonemic Awareness

Now, repeat this same process for each of the words below.

m-u-m   muuuuum   mum

t-u-x

b-u-t

m-u-d

p-u-t

c-u-p

l-u-ck

f-u-n

p-u-n

g-u-t

d-u-g

Phonemic Awareness

First, say each word. Next, ask students to (1) change the first letter of the word. Or (2) ask students to change the last letter of the word.

mum   (Ex. pum) (Ex. muck)
tux
but
mud
put
cup
luck
fun
pun
gut
dug

Words

Ask your student to read each of the words and sentences.

mum	off	luck
tux	gut	pun
fun	mud	cup

Sentences

1. Mum had a fun tux.
2. But mum fell in the mud.
3. The mud got on mum's gut.
4. Mum put the mud in a cup.
5. Mum had bad luck.
6. Mum had a fun mud pun.

Story

Mum had a fun tux. But mum fell in the mud. The mud got on mum's gut. Mum rubs the mud off. Mum put the mud in a cup. Mum gets up. Mum had bad luck. But mum had a fun mud pun.

Draw what happened in the story

Ask your student to read the following nonsense words from the box below. Though these are not real words, the goal is to get students to read them fluently and quickly. To accomplish this, you student may try as many times as possible within 3-5 minutes.

Silly Sentences

1. **tud, muf, pul, lus, wuc.**
2. **fum, sud, zug, pus, yun.**
3. **mux, yut, rus, gub, buc.**
4. **gup, gap, gop, gep.**
5. **vux, mun, dup, lum, kup.**
6. **dut, dus, yug, buf, wus.**

Ask your student to spell and write the following words: mum, fun, tux, gut, mud, pun.

Short u
Set 3

Phonemic Awareness

For this exercise, asks your student to blend each word together. Do not allow them to see any part of the word or book. This is an oral exercise.

Teacher: "Repeat after me.
b-u-g
buuuuuuug
bug"

(First, say each sound individually. Then, blend them together, dragging out the middle "u" sound. Next, say the word.)

Phonemic Awareness

Now, repeat this same process for each of the words below.

c-u-b   cuuub cun
s-u-b   suuub sub
n-u-t
b-u-g
b-u-s
y-u-m
y-u-p
u-s
p-u-p
u-p
h-u-n

Phonemic Awareness

First, say each word. Next, ask students to (1) change the first letter of the word. Or (2) ask students to change the last letter of the word.

cub   (Ex. dub) (Ex. cug)
sub
nut
bug
bus
yum
yup
us
pup
up
hun

Words

Ask your student to read each of the words and sentences.

cub	**nut**	**yup**
stuff	**bug**	**up**
sub	**yum**	**us**

Sentences

1. The cub is up on the bus.
2. The pup is in the sub.
3. Yup, the pup and cub get up on stuff.
4. The pup had gum.
5. The bug had gum.

Story

The cub is up on the bus. The pup is in the sub. Yup, the pup and cub get up on stuff. The pup had gum. The bug had gum. Yup, the cub and pup had gum in the sun. The pup and bug had nuts in the sun.

Draw what happened in the story

Ask your student to read the following nonsense words from the box below. Though these are not real words, the goal is to get students to read them fluently and quickly. To accomplish this, you student may try as many times as possible within 3-5 minutes.

Silly Sentences

1. **gus, gud, guf, guk, gub.**
2. **tus, tud, tuc, tuz, tut.**
3. **lup, lux, lus, luv, lub.**
4. **mun, mup, mul, muf.**
5. **hud, hul, huc, huk, hun.**
6. **juf, jum, jut, jup, jux.**

Ask your student to spell and write the following words: cub, pup, nut, sub, bus, yup.

Short u
Set 4

Phonemic Awareness

For this exercise, asks your student to blend each word together. Do not allow them to see any part of the word or book. This is an oral exercise.

Teacher: "Repeat after me.
b-u-g
buuuuuuug
bug"

(First, say each sound individually. Then, blend them together, dragging out the middle "u" sound. Next, say the word.)

Phonemic Awareness

Now, repeat this same process for each of the words below.

d-u-ck   duuuuck   duck
h-u-ck   huuuuck   huck
b-u-d
m-u-s-t
j-u-s-t
h-u-g-s
t-u-g-s
r-u-g
l-u-g-s
G-u-s-
b-u-t

Phonemic Awareness

First, say each word. Next, ask students to (1) change the first letter of the word. Or (2) ask students to change the last letter of the word.

duck   (Ex. ruck) (Ex. duf)
huck
bud
must
just
hugs
tugs
rug
lugs
Gus
but

Words

Ask your student to read each of the words and sentences.

duck	must	tug
huck	just	rug
bud	hugs	lug

Sentences

1. The duck has a fun bud.
2. The duck's bud is Gus.
3. The duck tugs the rug.
4. Gus lugs his bud the duck.
5. But the duck must hug Gus.

Story

The duck has a fun bud. The duck's bud is Gus. Gus and the duck must hug. But the duck is a bad bum. The duck tugs the rug. Gus lugs his bud the duck back to the hut. But the duck tugs a bug. The duck has fun. But Gus is mad at his bud.

Draw what happened in the story

Ask your student to read the following nonsense words from the box below. Though these are not real words, the goal is to get students to read them fluently and quickly. To accomplish this, you student may try as many times as possible within 3-5 minutes.

Silly Sentences

1. **guj, jav, rom, kev, fas.**
2. **pol, rux, caz, tep, lus.**
3. **yas, bup, lod, weg, tez.**
4. **nak, zel, ruv, jom, vat.**
5. **yel, rab, elc, uns, wug.**
6. **dun, vak, bex, huz, jov.**

Ask your student to spell and write the following words: fun, bud, Gus, lug, tug, bum.

Short u
Set 5

Phonemic Awareness

For this exercise, asks your student to blend each word together. Do not allow them to see any part of the word or book. This is an oral exercise.

Teacher: "Repeat after me.
b-u-g
buuuuuuug
bug"

(First, say each sound individually. Then, blend them together, dragging out the middle "u" sound. Next, say the word.)

Phonemic Awareness

Now, repeat this same process for each of the words below.

m-u-g   muuuug   mug
t-u-g   tuuuug   tug
m-u-s-t
b-u-s-t
p-u-g
r-u-b-s
n-u-t
h-u-b
d-u-g
b-u-t
m-u-d

Phonemic Awareness

First, say each word. Next, ask students to (1) change the first letter of the word. Or (2) ask students to change the last letter of the word.

mug   (Ex. rug) (Ex. mud)
tug
must
bust
pug
rubs
nut
hub
dug
but
mud

Words

Ask your student to read each of the words and sentences.

mug	bust	dug
pug	must	his
for	mud	rub

Sentences

1. The pug had his best mug.
2. The pug dug for bugs to put in his mug.
3. The pug must rub his mug.
4. The mug bust and mud runs to the hut.

Story

The pug had his best mug. The pug dug for nuts to put in his mug. But the pug put bugs in his mug. The pug must rub his mug. But the mug bust and the bugs run to the hut. The mug was cut. But the pug put up his mug and got a cup.

Draw what happened in the story

Ask your student to read the following nonsense words from the box below. Though these are not real words, the goal is to get students to read them fluently and quickly. To accomplish this, you student may try as many times as possible within 3-5 minutes.

Silly Sentences

1. **gub, mog, tuns, las, pec.**
2. **han, dus, fum, lep, hoc.**
3. **zob, suts, dast, bufs, vat.**
4. **fet, zen, wol, hup, zux.**
5. **haf, reg, huj, voz, mac.**
6. **yux, rem, puk, lum, yop.**

Ask your student to spell and write the following words: mug, cup, pug, mud, must, bust.

Short i
Set 1

Phonemic Awareness

For this exercise, asks your student to blend each word together. Do not allow them to see any part of the word or book. This is an oral exercise.

Teacher: "Repeat after me.
p-i-g
piiiiiiiiig
pig"

(First, say each sound individually. Then, blend them together, dragging out the middle "i" sound. Next, say the word.)

Phonemic Awareness- Blending

Now, repeat this same process for each of the words below.

p-i-t   piiiiiiit   pit
d-i-m   diiiiiim   dim
s-i-p
r-i-p
r-i-m
w-i-n
f-i-t
z-i-p
s-i-t
l-i-d
k-i-d

Phonemic Awareness

First, say each word. Next, ask students to (1) change the first letter of the word. Or (2) ask students to change the last letter of the word.

pit   (Ex. mit)   (Ex. pin)
dim
sip
rip
rim
win
fit
zip
sit
lid
kid

Words

Ask your student to read each of the words and sentences.

pig	bit	milk
pin	sips	sip
big	mix	in

Sentences

1. The pig is in the pig pen.
2. The pig has a sip of milk.
3. It is a big milk mix.
4. The milk has fig in it.
5. The pig bit the fig.

Story

The pig is in the pig pen. The pig has a sip of milk. It is a big milk mix. The milk has fig in it. The pig bit the fig. The fig said "yip, yip" as he had the fig and milk mix. The pig likes the mix. The pig thinks the mix is a big win.

Draw what happened in the story

Ask your student to read the following nonsense words from the box below. Though these are not real words, the goal is to get students to read them fluently and quickly. To accomplish this, you student may try as many times as possible within 3-5 minutes.

Silly Sentences

1. **mis, kib, fip, lim, vit.**
2. **din, wib, ric, sil, hig.**
3. **zim, vik, ril, giv, zid.**
4. **kix, fim, wil, vim, wid.**
5. **vig, rij, jit, yim, fid.**
6. **sis, bib, mim, pip, kik.**

Ask your student to spell and write the following words: pig, big, mix, yip, mix, milk.

Short i
Set 2

Phonemic Awareness

For this exercise, asks your student to blend each word together. Do not allow them to see any part of the word or book. This is an oral exercise.

Teacher: "Repeat after me.
p-i-g
piiiiiiiiig
pig"

(First, say each sound individually. Then, blend them together, dragging out the middle "i" sound. Next, say the word.)

Phonemic Awareness- Blending

Now, repeat this same process for each of the words below.

s-i-x   siiix   six
k-i-d   kiiid   kid
r-i-g
b-i-g
r-i-b
f-i-g
w-i-g
J-i-m
T-i-m
f-i-n
s-i-t

Phonemic Awareness

First, say each word. Next, ask students to (1) change the first letter of the word. Or (2) ask students to change the last letter of the word.

six
kid
rig
big
rib
fig
wig
Jim
Tim
fin
sit

Words

Ask your student to read each of the words and sentences.

six	**big**	**wig**
kid	**rig**	**Jim**
rig	**lunch**	**Tim**

Sentences

1. **Six kids sat in a big rig.**
2. **Jim, Tim, Liz, Pits, Inez, and Idell.**
3. **The six kid had six big wigs.**
4. **The six kids had figs and ribs for lunch.**

Story

Six kids sit in a big rig. Jim, Tim, Liz, Pits, Inez, and Idell. The six kids had six big wigs. The six kids with big wigs had figs and ribs for lunch. Tim hid from Pits and Liz. But Inez saw Tim sit in a dim bin. The six kids got off the rig.

Draw what happened in the story

Ask your student to read the following nonsense words from the box below. Though these are not real words, the goal is to get students to read them fluently and quickly. To accomplish this, you student may try as many times as possible within 3-5 minutes.

Silly Sentences

1. bis, vim, nid, sij, lik.
2. wib, wic, siz, hix, rit.
3. hiz, ril, sid, lib, hiv.
4. miv, mav, mov, muv, mev.
5. lis, las, los, lus, les.
6. tif, pif, mif, nif, gif, dif.

Ask your student to spell and write the following words: six, kid, sit, big, rig, Pits.

Short i
Set 3

Phonemic Awareness

For this exercise, asks your student to blend each word together. Do not allow them to see any part of the word or book. This is an oral exercise.

Teacher: "Repeat after me.
p-i-g
piiiiiiiiig
pig"

(First, say each sound individually. Then, blend them together, dragging out the middle "i" sound. Next, say the word.)

Phonemic Awareness- Blending

Now, repeat this same process for each of the words below.

L-i-z
r-i-b-s
h-i-t
t-i-n
l-i-p
z-i-p
l-i-d
k-i-t
z-i-t
r-i-m
k-i-n

Phonemic Awareness

First, say each word. Next, ask students to (1) change the first letter of the word. Or (2) ask students to change the last letter of the word.

Liz

ribs

hit

tin

lip

zip

lid

kit

zit

rim

kin

Words

Ask your student to read each of the words and sentences.

Liz	tin	home
passed	lid	kin
ribs	zips	kit

Sentences

1. Liz hit her ribs and lip on a tin lid.
2. Liz zips passed the bin and sees her kin Jim.
3. Jim helps Liz with her hit ribs and lip.

Story

Liz hit her ribs and lip on a tin lid. Liz zips passed the bin and sees her kin Jim. Jim has a kit to help Liz. Jim helps Liz with her hit ribs and lip. Jim and Liz zips passed the tin bin. Liz and Jim go home.

Draw what happened in the story

Ask your student to read the following nonsense words from the box below. Though these are not real words, the goal is to get students to read them fluently and quickly. To accomplish this, you student may try as many times as possible within 3-5 minutes.

Silly Sentences

1. kix, ziv, tig, miv, pid, hif.
2. wim, rif, jik, zic, vil, vis.
3. div, bip, vix, div, mif.
4. mits, rill, lins, ilp, ild.
5. ivs, igs, zilp, bilt, sift.
6. jits, hids, sills, vist, bif.

Ask your student to spell and write the following words: Liz, kin, lip, tin, hit, lid.

Short i
Set 4

Phonemic Awareness

For this exercise, asks your student to blend each word together. Do not allow them to see any part of the word or book. This is an oral exercise.

Teacher: "Repeat after me.
p-i-g
piiiiiiiiig
pig"

(First, say each sound individually. Then, blend them together, dragging out the middle "i" sound. Next, say the word.)

Phonemic Awareness- Blending

Now, repeat this same process for each of the words below.

y-i-p
h-i-p
d-i-d
w-i-t
qu-i-ck
p-i-t
z-i-g
h-i-d
w-i-n
f-i-n
d-i-p

Phonemic Awareness

First, say each word. Next, ask students to (1) change the first letter of the word. Or (2) ask students to change the last letter of the word.

yip
hip
did
wit
quick
pit
zig
hid
win
fin
dip

Words

Ask your student to read each of the words and sentences.

Sid	zig	into
win	did	wit
race	zip	dip

Sentences

1. Sid had a race to run.
2. Sid zips into a big pit.
3. Next, Sid zips by six bins.
4. Sid has quick wits.
5. He did win the race.

Story

Sid had a big race to run. Sid has a big list of six wins he has to get. Sid zips into a big pit. Next, Sid zips by six bins. Sid is quick. Sid has quick wits. Sid did win the race. Sid said, "Yip yip. Hip, hip."

Draw what happened in the story

Ask your student to read the following nonsense words from the box below. Though these are not real words, the goal is to get students to read them fluently and quickly. To accomplish this, you student may try as many times as possible within 3-5 minutes.

Silly Sentences

1. **dis, das, dos, dus, des.**
2. **mag, meg, mig, mog, mug.**
3. **fim, fem, fom, fam, fum.**
4. **zut, zat, zet, zot, zit.**
5. **pel, pal, pil, pul, pol.**

Ask your student to spell and write the following words: Sid, win, did, is, yip, hip.

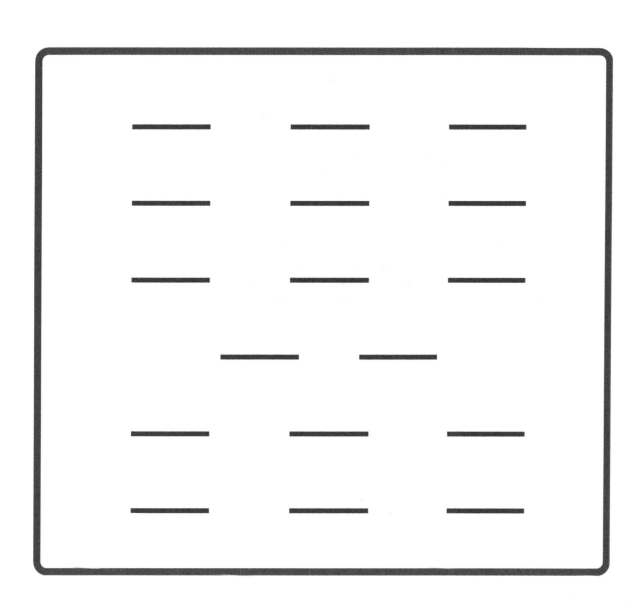

Short i
Set 5

Phonemic Awareness

For this exercise, asks your student to blend each word together. Do not allow them to see any part of the word or book. This is an oral exercise.

Teacher: "Repeat after me.
p-i-g
piiiiiiiiig
pig"

(First, say each sound individually. Then, blend them together, dragging out the middle "i" sound. Next, say the word.)

Phonemic Awareness- Blending

Now, repeat this same process for each of the words below.

V-i-n
b-i-b
i-n
i-s
i-f
i-t
t-i-p
p-i-g
l-i-ck
p-i-ck
J-i-ll

Phonemic Awareness

First, say each word. Next, ask students to (1) change the first letter of the word. Or (2) ask students to change the last letter of the word.

Vin

bib

in

is

if

it

tip

pig

lick

pick

Jill

Words

Ask your student to read each of the words and sentences.

Jill	tip	in
ibis	lick	licks
bib	pick	it

Sentences

1. **Jill the ibis has six red bibs.**
2. **Jill licks a tick in the pit.**
3. **Jill picks it up in a bin.**
4. **Jill tips the bin back in the pit.**
5. **The Ibis got rid of the tick.**

Story

Jill the ibis has six red bibs. Jill licks a tick in the pit. Jill picks it up in a bin. Jill tips the bin back in the pit. The Ibis got rid of the tick. Jill rips the bin and put it in the pit. Jill was bad. But Jill put the tick back on land and left.

Draw what happened in the story

Ask your student to read the following nonsense words from the box below. Though these are not real words, the goal is to get students to read them fluently and quickly. To accomplish this, you student may try as many times as possible within 3-5 minutes.

Silly Sentences

1. rix, rax, tix, tax, gix, gax.
2. lop, jav, muf, gaf, zif.
3. tid, miz, lil, viv, wis.
4. riz, vim, raz, vam, vuz, vam.
5. tol, til, tal, tel, tul.
6. ut, it, at, ot, et.

Ask your student to spell and write the following words: bib, tip, picks, Jill, Ibis, tick, pick.

Thank You

Congratulations to all the parents and teachers who have successfully completed book one of our Science of Reading curriculum! Your dedication and commitment to guiding young readers through this essential phase of their literacy development are truly commendable. By completing book one, you have laid a solid foundation for building strong and confident readers, equipped with the necessary phonemic awareness, phonics, and decoding skills to tackle more complex texts with ease. Your efforts have undoubtedly set the stage for a future filled with academic success and a lifelong love for reading.

As you celebrate this milestone achievement, we encourage you to look forward to the journey ahead with excitement and anticipation. Book two of our curriculum promises to delve deeper into the intricacies of literacy instruction, further enhancing your child's reading abilities and nurturing their passion for learning. Together, let us continue to empower our young readers, providing them with the tools and support they need to thrive in an ever-changing world. Thank you for your unwavering commitment to the success of your children and students. We cannot wait to see the incredible progress they will continue to make in book two and beyond.

CERTIFICATE
OF COMPLETION

This Certificate is proudly presented to

_____

For mastering short vowel sounds

PRESENTED BY

_____

Made in United States
Cleveland, OH
21 March 2025

15364806R00129